Famatta
youre beautiful
youre doing great

Kelly Rae

Little Girl Lost

Five years ago
God called home
A beautiful baby girl
She was a very sick
20 month old baby girl
Who defeated all odds
And stayed with us
Longer than expected
Your momma misses you
Cedie Bug
Your grand-parents do too
I hope you watch over them
Every now and then
And come visit sometimes
To see the wonderful
Inspirational woman
Your momma is today
Keep watch over her
And everyone else
Be sure to use those legs
We hardly got to see you use
And tell God all your stories
With the beautiful voice
We rarely got to hear
It's a shame
You didn't get to see the world
Rest in Peace baby girl

No Love

Who are you
When I'm not around
Where have you been
Only gets answered with
"around"
What if that's not good enough
I want to know where you've been
I really could have used a friend
These past couple of years
Yes, I have other friends
But there was something about you
You always knew just what to say
To make everything Okay
After a while you decided
You needed some space
One of the things
You cut out of your life
Was me
That's the day I realized
There was no love lost
And there was no love found

Running

What are you looking for
“nothing” is the common response
But what about the people
Who are looking for some thing
The ones that are always running
What about them
Where do they fit in this world
Everyone says just be yourself
And you won’t have to run
What if the people who are running
Don’t know who they are
Sometimes you run
Not because
Of not knowing who you are
But because
Being that person scares you
So you run until you can face them
Sometimes that involves
Never looking back
While sometimes
You’re forced to
Running doesn’t get you very far
In terms of
Finding out who you truly are
Because sooner or later
You have to stop
Or risk losing out on life

Murder of a young Boy

You kill him out of pleasure
I kill you out of pain
What would that solve
What would anybody gain
You hurt a lot of people
I bet you don't even care
I hope you have fun in jail
I hope people treat you like dirt
And when you get out
Or if you get out
I hope you got satisfaction
Out of ruining people's lives
Because if you get out
Your family will still have you
Your friends can still call you
But Zach's family doesn't
And his friends have to go
To a gravesite to visit him
You shouldn't have killed him
It was just a video game
He was 15
You were 17
Why did you have a gun
Why did you have to kill him

Free

You killed him out of pleasure
So we killed you out of pain
8 ½ years ago
You took Zach from us
Yet you somehow managed
To only be in prison
For not even 4 years
How is that fair
You took someone's life
Who was only 15
And you spent
Not even a third of that
Locked up
You better enjoy your freedom
While you can
One day
You'll get what you deserve
Haven't you heard of Karma
You just got released
And already
You are a wanted fugitive
We should've killed you
When we had the chance
Then maybe Zach
Could finally be free

Death

You died to show your love
To a girl who had no clue
She meant the world to you
But you never told her
She misses you every day
But you don't know that
Because you are dead
You should have told her
How you felt
You didn't have to die to prove
You were in love with her
She was certain that you were
It's been 3 years
She never forgot your face
And until she's dead and buried
She will love you unconditionally

You

You left me
Sad and all alone
Don't you know
I love you
The day you died
I was not there
I was at home
Having a good time
Maybe if I would
Have been there
You'd still be alive
Many nights I lie awake
Thinking about you
And ways I could have helped
Why didn't you tell me
Or anyone that you were sad
We could have gotten you help
If only you let us
You hurt a lot of people
You don't even know
You couldn't even imagine
But just remember
When you're up In Heaven
I love you
And I always will

Best Friend

You are my best friend
Through thick and thin
You make new friends
I make new friends
When Nick died
You were there
When Aaron died
I was there
I was there when
Your parents were having problems
You were there
When I was having problems
You mean more to me
Than anyone ever could
I hope you know
You can always call me
No matter what
I love you Kristin
I always have and I always will
You are my best friend
Through thick and thin

Do You Believe me Now

I miss you
And I love you
But when I tell you that
You seem to question it
I've never given you
Any reason to doubt me
We were best friends
I know you miss it
Because I do too
You say it all the time
And at first I questioned it too
I think I did that
Because I didn't want to believe it
Even though I knew it was true
So after everything
That has happened between us
How is it
That I can manage
To believe you
But you can't seem to manage
To believe me
We started talking more
And one thing led to another
So do you believe me now

Untitled

Staring out this window
While this storm goes through
Makes me stop and wonder
Why the skies are so blue
Why do we have
The storms that we do
What is it supposed to teach
When a tree gets uprooted
And falls on a house
Why do you let that happen
Or when that tornado
Ripped through my town
What is your plan
It seems like these things happen
More than they should
But how do you take something so bad
And turn it in to something good

Gone

Gone are the days
Of us being friends
Gone are the days
Of us even talking
It's been three years
Since the last time we talked
Now you want back in
Why
Why now
We were best friends
You told me secrets
And I told you secrets
Then three years and nothing
You know how bad that hurt
Then I got over it
And never thought of you again
You say you want to be friends again
Like we used to be
But I don't know if I can do that
Because I refuse to get hurt again

A Tribute to Aaron and Seth

It's been two years
Since your untimely deaths
But no one has ever forgot
About you or the tragedy
I'm sorry for what happened
I wish it would have been me
Instead of the two of you
Aaron, your life was ended
After 17 short years
And Seth,
Yours ended after only 14
Hopefully you guys
Can Rest in Peace
Knowing Jason is locked up
And will never get out
You are missed everyday
By people that you didn't know
And by people that you did
No one will ever forget the tragedy
And they will never forget
The two great guys that died
That horrible September day

Time Goes by Fast

Six years ago today
The world lost two amazing young men
Aaron Rollins and Seth Bartell
Aaron was 17
Seth was 14
And they were taken from us
In one of the worst ways
And I am so sorry for that
I never met Seth
But my best friend knew Aaron
And I met him a few times
I can't relate to losing a child
At the hands of another person
I think about that day
Every day and will for the rest of my life
To Aaron and Seth's parents
Know that your sons
Touched many people's lives
And they will never be forgotten

Judgment

Why do you judge
Does it make you feel better
So what if I don't look like you
I dress different then you
I wear my hair different then you
What right does that give you
Are you against individuality
Or do you feel so insecure with yourself
That you have to judge people
I find it ironic
How you claim to be so happy
Yet you have to judge people
While I am truly happy
Not listening to haters like you
I am me
You either like me or you don't
Either way
I don't care
I have my friends
Who have been my friends for years
And I am okay
If who I am
Interferes with who you want to be

4 Years

You talk about your feelings
How you still love me
How you miss me
How you still want me
We didn't talk for
4 years
Now all of a sudden
You want a second chance
But it's too late for all that
You had
4 years
Where were you during that time
Where were you when I needed you
Too busy for me
Or did you just not care
You had
4 years
To tell me how you felt
And you said nothing
I'm sorry if I hurt you
But how was I supposed to know
You made your choice
And now you have to live with it
For years

Love to my Momma

You can't change the past
You can only live for today
And hope for tomorrow
I know you have regrets
About things you wish
Could have been different
But life is way too short
To live with regrets and what if's
Everything happens for a reason
We may not know what it is
Or fully agree with it
But God has a plan for everything
So please stop blaming yourself
And thinking you are a bad momma
Because I don't blame you
And I think you're a great momma
So live for today
Hope for tomorrow
And forget about the past
That stuff doesn't matter

Untitled

So many questions
Left unanswered
Why
I have often wondered
There are things I want
To say to you
Things that are
Way over due
Sometimes you question
What I say
And make me feel
Like I should just go away
This friendship is not
How it used to be
Is there something there
That we don't see
You've changed a lot
And so have I
I wonder if
We should say good-bye
Good-bye to whom
We used to be
Good-bye to whom
We will never be
Sometimes I wish
There was a way
We could go back
To the old days
Before the fight
Before we drifted apart
Before talking to you
Was this hard
I miss you
I really do

But I’m not sure
If we can be as close
As we were back then
You don’t talk to me
Like you used to
You answer questions with
“cause” or “dunno”
What happened to
Being able to talk to me
Like we did all those summers
At the beach
I feel like I lost
One of my best friends
Who doesn’t even care
If this friendship ends
So it’s up to you
Do we stay friends
Or is this
The end

Secrets

Everyone has secrets
Some you share
Some you don't
But you know those ones
Way down deep inside
Those are meant to stay inside
If your secret involves someone
And you know
That if you told that secret
It could ruin their life
Why would you threaten to do that
You say you love them
And don't want to hurt them
But you're not acting
Like you don't want to hurt them
The best way to lose a friend
Is to tell their secrets

Trust

Trust is such a hard thing to get
But once you get it
It is the greatest feeling
But lose it
And you can never get it back
You lost my trust
And now you want it back
I said I would work on it
So why would you want to ruin that
Do you not care
You say you care
But yet you dare
To throw my trust away
If you don't want to be friends
Then get out of my life
Because I'm not going to have you
Coming in
Then going out
Over and over
You're either in or out
You can't be both

Why

When someone says they love you
Why do they normally not mean it
Many people don't know the definition
Of what love is
What they do have
Is the definition
Of what they think love is
Some definitions are good
While some are bad
A good one is a guy
Giving a girl flowers to show her he cares
A bad one is a guy
Who beats his girlfriend because
That is what his dad did to his mom
So that's what he thought guys did
To show a female they love them
To show me you love me
Buy me flowers
Take me to a movie
But do not beat me
The night you did that
I lost all respect for guys
Luckily, I have met some great guys since then
Who don't disrespect me
To show me that they care
Do you know what sucks though
Even though they don't disrespect me
I still have trouble trusting them
All because a guy told me he loved me
And showed it by beating me

The Best Present

The best present of all is life
It is one gift that cannot be returned
However
It is one that can be taken away
Why would someone do that
Why would you take something
That isn't yours
How could you take
Somebody's life
Don't you feel any remorse
Don't you think about their family
And how much pain you caused them
How could anyone in their right mind
Take another human's life
The best present is life
And you took that present away
Not just from one person
But from a city
A community
I just have one question for you
How could you take another human's life

Hurt

Nothing can ever replace the pain
That I have been dealt
If there is a God
And he does everything for a reason
Why has he put me through hell
If there is a past life
What did I do to deserve this
But then I met you
I felt I had finally done something
That must have been great
To get a man like you
You are yet to cause me pain
Every time I'm with you I have fun
Even though it may seem like I don't
Believe it or not I do
I know when I'm in a bad mood
I may seem like a Bitch
But you should know by now
That when I'm happy
Nothing can bring me down
I like that you make me happy
I feel safe when I'm with you
Please don't ever hurt me
Because I will never hurt you

To Katrina

You know you're right
The rain in my sky
Are the tears from my eyes
And the pain in my heart
Is from people in my past
You say you are worried
But you don't do anything
Except yell at me
Have you ever thought
That yelling doesn't help
That I'll continue doing it
Just when you're not around
I have a problem
Cutting is a problem
A serious one at that
You think I want to cut
That I do it just for fun
Because I don't
I do it because
I don't know what else to do
You say I can talk to you
But I can't put in to words
The pain that I am feeling
So I tell my pain through my actions
I don't know any other way
I want to be able to talk
But I don't trust anybody
Maybe that's my problem too

How Could You

How could you do this
How could you hurt me
You told me you loved me
When I asked if you meant it
You said with your whole heart
You told me I have a high guard
And that I should let it down
That you were different
And that you would never hurt me
But those were all lies
I let it down
And you proved you were the same
You don't know what you want
You don't care about anyone
I never understood you
You were such a jerk to me
I never understood how a female
Could be in an abusive relationship
And not leave the guy
Unfortunately, now I do
You verbally abused me Matt
You physically abused me
And you emotionally abused me
I'm glad you are hurt
That I moved on and am happy
It's sad you don't know
What you want in a relationship
And out of life
But I'm not sorry
That I moved on
You only liked me
So you could say you had a girlfriend
I hope one day
You figure out what you want

And when that day comes
Don't think about me
Don't call me
Cause I won't care anymore
And if you do think of me
Think about how I'm with someone else
And I'm happy and enjoying life
Then think to yourself
"Damn, I just lost a great girl"

Always be Yourself

I live my life one day at a time
Many people don't understand that
I don't plan my days or my weekends
Whatever happens, happens
Why can't you understand that
Why is it so hard to realize
What I do is what I do
So why do you care
I don't care what people think
It's pointless and a waste of time
If I care what you think
I would be living to your expectations
And not my own
Isn't life stressful enough
To deal with our own problems
Then to care what other people think
Be yourself
It's the best way to be
You are much happier that way
Living up to what other people think
Would get tiring
You wouldn't be yourself then
You would be constantly changing
Because their opinion would change
That's not who you are
If you want to change something
It should be because you want to
And not because someone told you to
Or because their opinion changed
That is why you should be yourself
And not care what other people think
Don't you have better things to do
And spend your time on
Then caring what people think of you

Watch what you Say

Sometimes we say things
We don't really mean
But words hurt people
And once they are said
You can never take them back
So be careful
And watch the things
That comes out of your mouth
Because what you think is a joke
Someone may take serious
So if you mean it as a joke
Say it in a joking manner
And don't point it at one person
If you do end up hurting someone
Make sure they know
That it wasn't intentional
And that you are sorry
Hurting them was never your intention
So watch what you say
You would never want
The last thing you say to someone
To be a bad memory

I'm Done

I'm done letting the past
Affect the present
And I'm not going to let it
Affect the future
I'm done ruining things
That are great
Because I can't let go
Of things in my past
I hate everyone
And love a few
But I'm done now
I refuse to ruin this
It's too great of a thing
He doesn't deserve it
He's too great of a guy
I'm starting over
I'm not going to judge him
By the assholes in my past
It's not his fault
So why take my anger out on him
People can say what they want
But from now on
I'm going to live everyday
Like it should be
Every day is a brand new day
The past is the past
And I can't change anything from it
But I can change
How I deal with it
Things happen
That's just how life is
But you can't blame those people
Who have nothing to do with it
I love him and I'm not going to let

My unhappy past
Ruin my happiness with him
Now or in the future

Thinking of you at Night

I lie awake at night
Thinking about you
And how it isn't fair
It shouldn't have been you
You had no reason to die
You loved life
And life loved you
You always had a smile on your face
No matter what you were going through
You had a great life
And too many friends to count
The day you died
A part of everyone who knew you
Died too
I wrote a poem for you
And it was read at your memorial service
So many people want revenge
But I know that is not what you would want
You would want us to forgive
And let him deal with his own demons
But that is so hard to do sometimes
I want you to know
We all love you
And miss you
Life will never be the same
Without you in it
But know that your memory lives on
In things that we say
And things that we do
We want you to be proud of us
As we are of you
No one will ever forget you
Because everyone has memories
And we will meet again

Caleb

You wrote they tell you jail is your destiny
But you don't have to listen
Because you are the type of person
Who will always glisten
You are such a great person
Sometimes you do some bad things
You never have to worry about falling
There is someone below you with wings
Ready to push you back up
Whenever you take a fall
You never have to worry
For you will never hit a brick wall
You can be whatever you want to be
The limit is as high as the sky
And you never have to worry
Your true friends will never say good-bye
We are with you all the time
One day you will see
For now, picture us in your head
And there we will always be

Two roads in Life

You have two roads in life
You can either take the high road
That leads to school
Lets you get a good job
Get married and have children
Or you can take the low road
That leads to drug use
Alcohol addiction and eventually death
I chose to take the high road
Why you ask
Because I want to do something with my life
You took the low road
Why I ask
I'm never going to get an answer
Because your life ended
When you were only 17

Drugs

I always told myself
I would never do drugs
That it wasn't worth my time
That it was just for thugs
But then one night
When I was sixteen
My brother asked me
One simple thing
He asked me if
I've ever done Cocaine
Now it seems
I can't feel my pain
I became addicted
Since the first time I tried
What is wrong with me
I feel like I should have tried
Harder and stuck to my guns
About never doing drugs
Because now I'm just a bum

Navy

Many people are nervous
About joining the Military
Not so much about Boot Camp
But what comes after
For many people that is War
War scares a lot of people
But then there are those
Like my friends and I
Who want to join
For the benefits it gives
Nothing about the Navy
Makes me think twice
Every day that passes
Is one closer to Boot Camp
And I embrace each day
With a smile
The day I get out
Will be one of the happiest
Because that would mean
That one of my dreams
Has been accomplished

You act like you don't know Me

You act like you don't know me
Whenever she's around
But when she's not
You act like everything is fine
I know you think I'm sweet
Quit being stupid and admit
To yourself and to me
That you have feelings for me
You mean a lot to me
You say I mean a lot to you
But whenever she's around
You change
The voice in my head
Says I should forget about you
My friends say the same thing
But I don't listen to them
I tell them they don't know
Maybe they're right
Maybe I'm wrong
You never let me forget
The say we kissed
You said it changed you
But it didn't
You still act like you don't know me
Whenever she's around
Why do you have to change
Why can't you stay the same

TJ

I never once met you
But I feel like I've known you forever
When you were with Kristin
She was always smiling
It was the happiest I'd ever seen her
When you went to Iraq
We all thought you were going to propose
But you didn't
Do you know how miserable she was
That girl was mad in love with you
And she still is
I wish you could have been here
To see how much she truly cared
It's not her fault you did what you did
And if you blame her
Then you don't deserve her
Because all she did was love you
Maybe if you weren't
Doing the drugs that you were
You'd still be here
Nothing in life is worth
Taking your own life
Do you know how many people
You hurt by doing that
You don't know me
But I'm hurt
Because my best friend
Blames herself
But you know it's not her fault
And I know that
But I'm not sure if she knows that
Many people don't know what to say to her
I tell her what I was told
When my boyfriend killed himself

I don’t know why you did it
But you could have asked for help
Anyone would have helped
If it would save a life

How I Feel

You told me you loved me
I believed it was true
But now I am sitting here crying
In part because of you
I gave you my heart
And what did you do
You seem to not believe me
When I say I love you
I know I'm different
Than the ones in your past
You never said that
But I know it's a fact
I want this to work
Really I do
Because believe it or not
I do love you
I'm scared to get too close
That I may lose you
I want us to work out
But honestly do you
I know I write a lot
And that I should talk
But no one ever gave me the time
They just got up and walked
But I don't want you to
I want to be able to explain
Things that I say and do
But most of the time I refrain
Everything happens for a reason
So there is a reason we met
And we got together
We just don't know it yet
With every passing day
I realize how happy I am

That we met that day
And a part of my life you became
If you want to read what I write
One day maybe I'll let you
With the hope that it will help
You not be so confused
I wish there was a way
I could prove to you
How much I really do
Love you
I like all the time
That we have spent together
And I've thought about
What it would be like
To be with you forever

Waiting

You say you are going to call me
That was three days ago
What is taking so long
Why haven't you called
My friends are starting to tell me things
Things like they have seen you
Walking with another girl
And kissing her in public
I am being totally faithful
I thought you were too
Then I hear all these things
About some girl and you
You told me you were being faithful
And I believed you
You told me you would never lie
But when I asked about her
You told me I was the only girl
When you finally do call
I asked you where you've been
And you say "out with the fellas"
You ask me to come over
So I said yes and started walking that way
When I get there I see you
You are with her
She came over to surprise you
And you must have forgot about me
Because I saw you two kissing

Untitled

I saw you over there
Talking to your friends
Holding a big stuffed bear
Like it's a new fashion trend
You laugh like you never want to stop
You smile like it's your favorite thing
You even laughed at a cop
Who was wearing a huge diamond ring
We've never met
But I know you felt it
When your friends made a bet
For you to do a silly skit
The next time you saw me
To try and be funny
But that will never be
Because you aren't that funny
I used to talk to my friends
About this person I like
So I made a new trend
Like riding a bike
All I want to do
Is meet you one day
Possibly take you to the zoo
And finally have it my way

Love of a young Girl

I'm sitting here thinking
While I'm babysitting
About you and how
I haven't been fitting
In to your busy life
You say you are my best friend
Well what do you know
Right now I'm all alone
You think I'm crazy
But I don't care
I am looking at all these pictures
And I'm about to tear
Them up and throw them away
I love you more
Than life itself
But I could never
Tell you this
It's ten 'o'clock at night
And I'm still babysitting
But still my thoughts
Are all about you
I met you back
In the seventh grade
And we became best friends
You told me to call you
But I never did
I told you to call me
But you never did
Now I am wondering
What is going on between us
You see
A girl's first love
Hardly ever escapes her mind
Even after many years

And relationships
A first love stays with you forever
So know that
No matter where you are
Or where I am
The love of a girl
You will always have

How do you get so Lonely

It was just another day
The same as the day before
I was sitting at home
And reading the daily newspaper
The Obituary section to be exact
And this one catches me eye
It's for a fourteen your old boy
It says he died tragically
He took his own life
What happened to this boy
To make him end his life
I stop and think
Think about you
And how it's been four years
And we still don't have any answers
And I don't think we ever will
We can ask as many questions as we want
But we will never get the answers
How did you get so lonely
That you took your own life
Did you get in a fight
With your parents or a friend
Did a girl break up with you
Maybe it was a long battle
With drugs or alcohol
Do you think we don't care
Or that we don't miss you
Because we do care
And we will always miss you
There is so much I wish I could tell you
But all I can do is look at pictures
And talk to you that way
Or I can write
And leave it at your gravesite

Lost Children

You did not die in vain
Your life was taken from you
By a monster
You will be missed everyday
By people you didn't even know
The country mourns for you
As this day
Will live in history
You will never be forgot
I've never heard of Newtown
The circumstances
Around how I hear about it
For the first time
Breaks my heart
Many people wonder
Who could do this
Who is this person
This Adam Lanza
What was wrong with him
That he would walk in to
A kindergarten class
And just start shooting
Dear children
Know that we love you
We are here for your family
And you did not die in vain

Ultimate Sacrifice

I thought of you
Today and yesterday too
I thought about the past
And things that didn't last
I thought about the present
And how you are so absent
I thought about the future
And how you'd make such a good suitor
But you left this world
Before you were that old
You future was taken from you
There was nothing we could do
We miss you every day
And wish you didn't go away
Your memory will never fade
Because of what you paid
You paid the Ultimate Sacrifice
And laid down your life
For something you believed in
But here
Nobody wins
I hope you Rest in Peace
Knowing you didn't leave
Because you wanted to
But because God chose you
I love you

Made in the USA
Monee, IL
14 August 2022

11573627R00031